Color and Trace the Letters of the Alphabet

This Coloring book belongs to :

____

ABC
Animal
Coloring Book

Millard Garcia

3

Copyright © 2020 coloringbooks

A

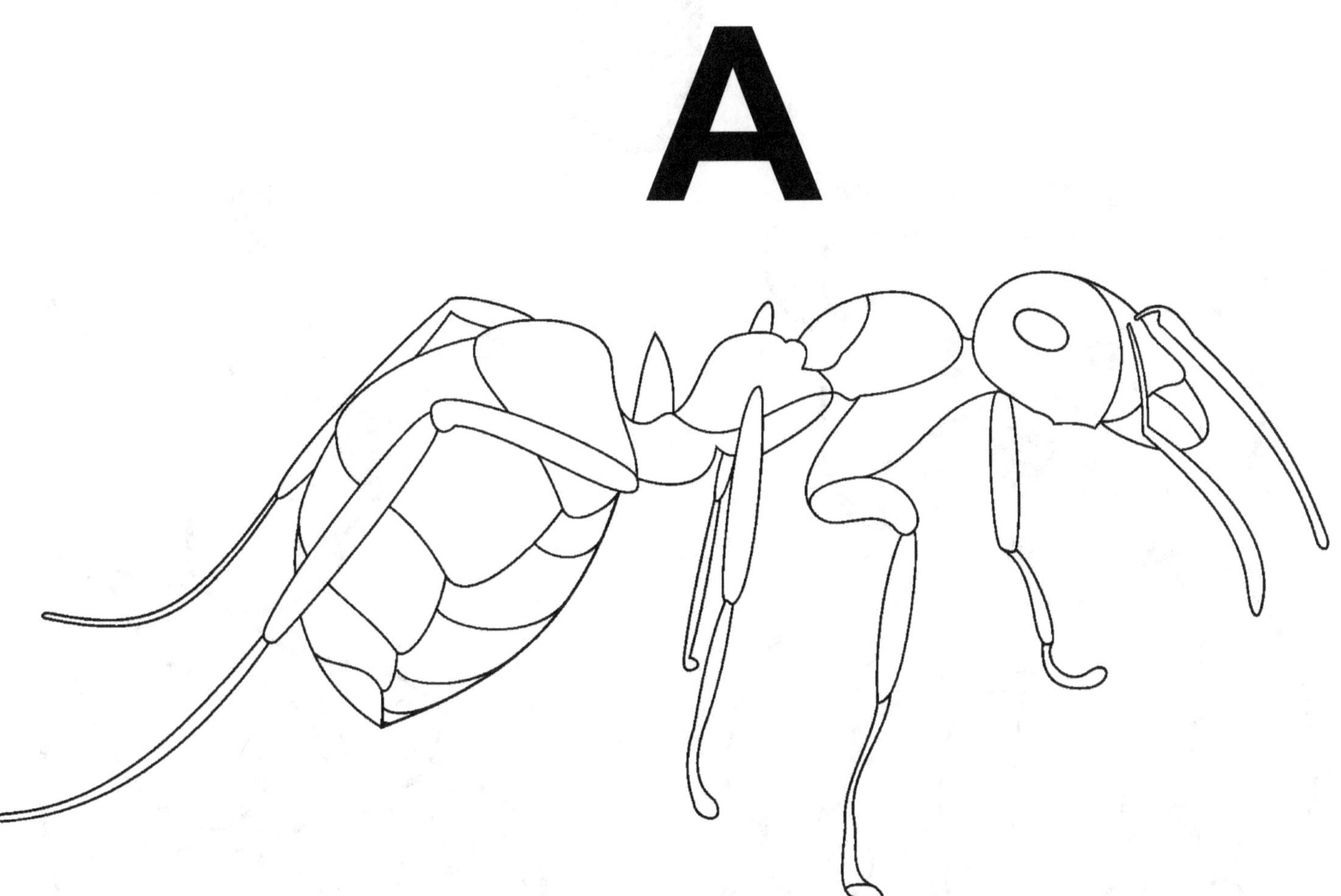

Ant

B

Bear

C

Cat

D

Dog

E

Eagle

F

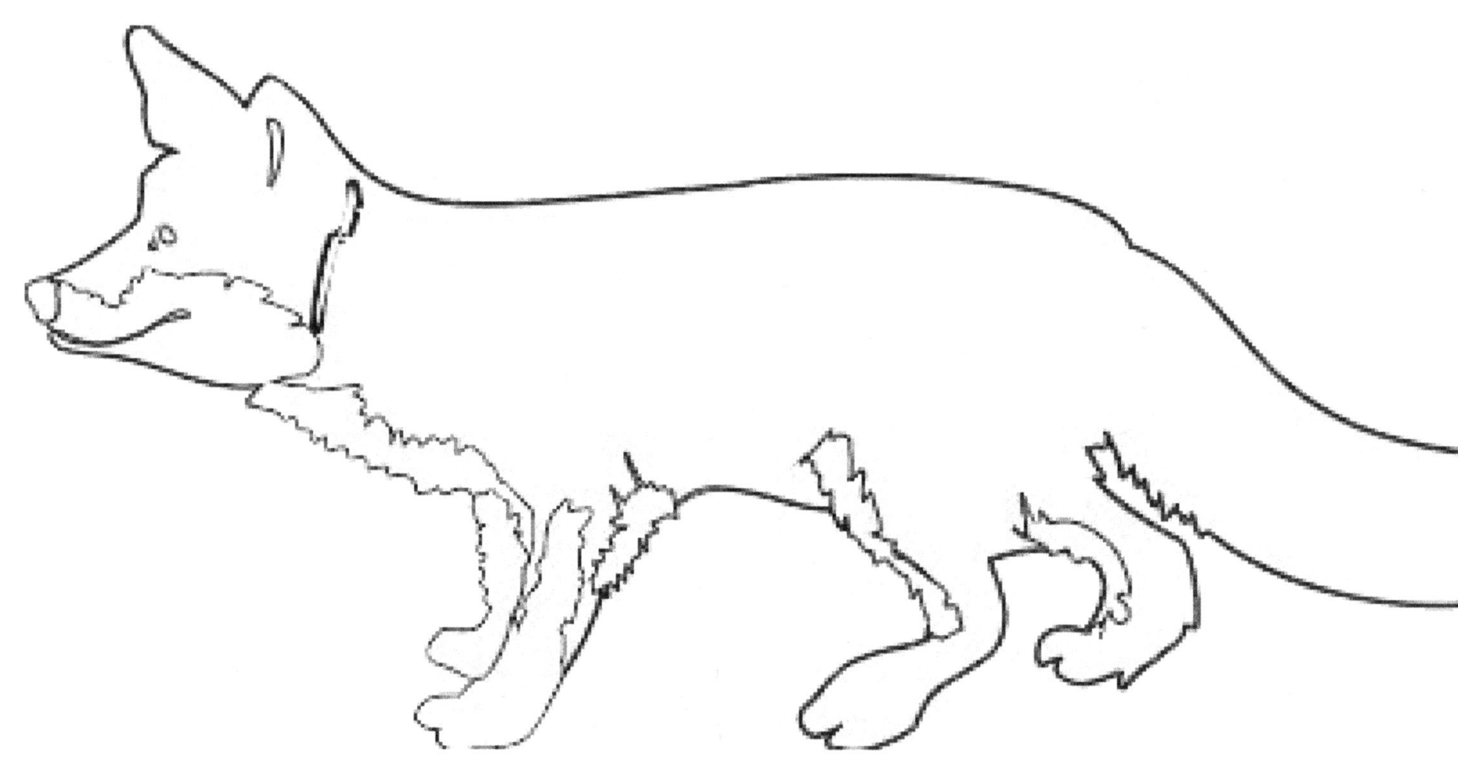

Fox

G

Goat

H

Horse

I

Iguana

J

Jellyfish

K

kangaroo

L

Lion

M

Mouse

N

Newt

O

Owl

P

Pig

Q

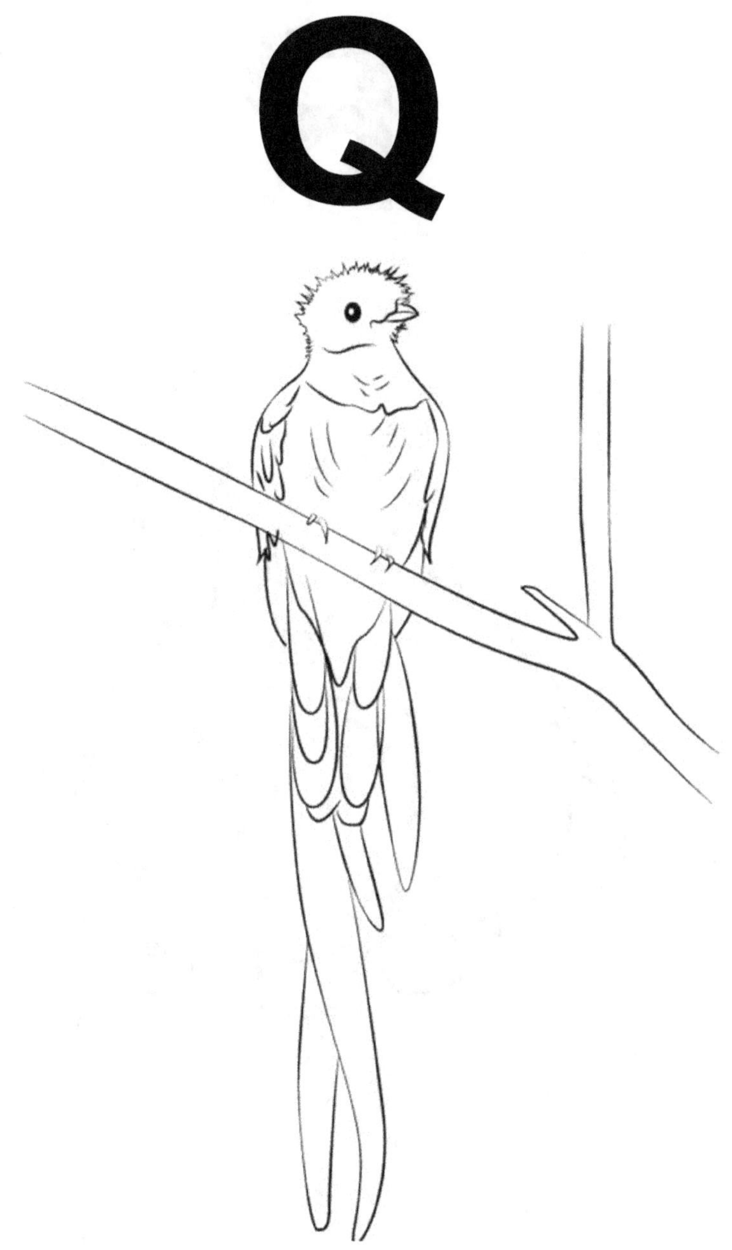

Quetzal

R

Rabbit

S

Shark

T

Turtle

U

Umbrellabird

V

Vulture

W

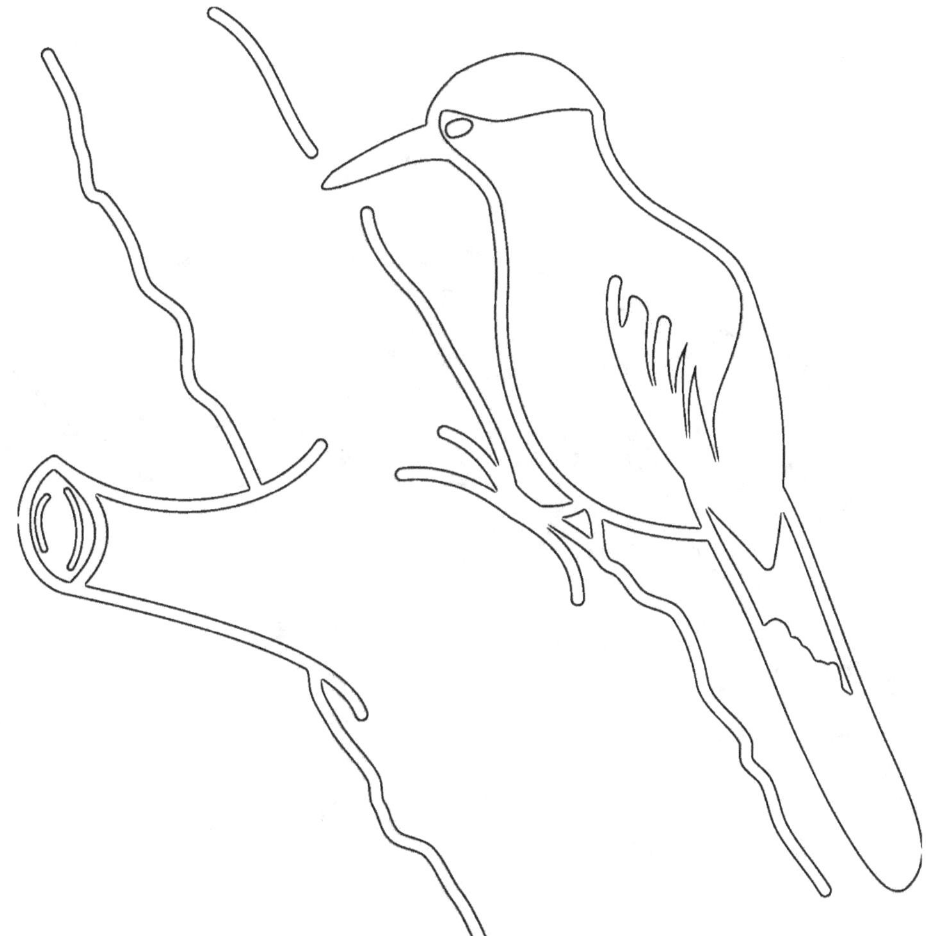

Woodpecker

X

X-Ray Tetra

Y

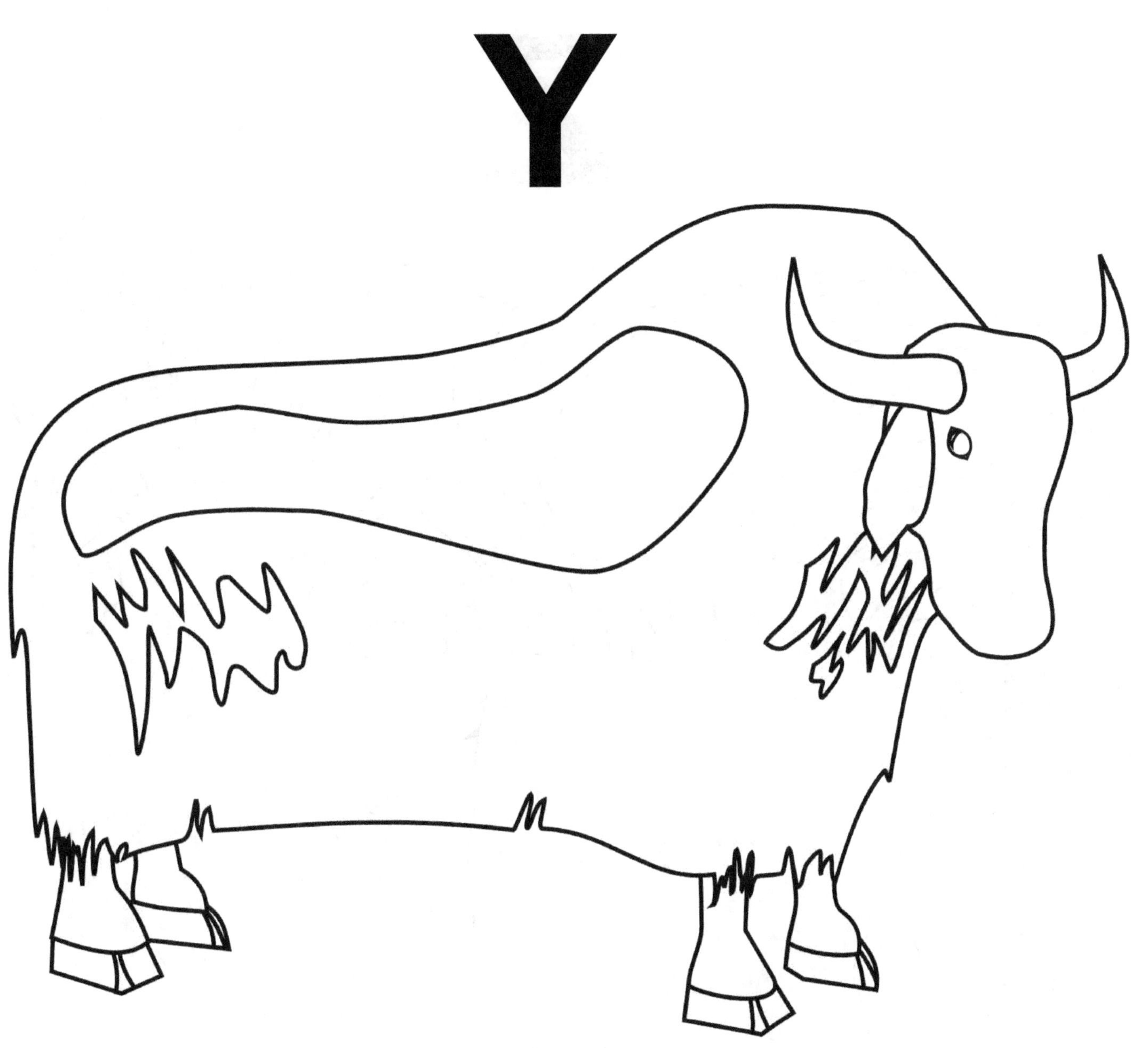

Yak

Z

Zebra

Practice Painting

Thank you for buying my book